Korky Paul

BIOGRAPHY OF AN ILLUSTRATOR

D0544174

Teresa Heapy

For all my family. K.P.

For Dad. T.H.

Acknowledgements

Illustrations
Korky Paul's private collection: title page, left; page 6, top and bottom; page 7, bottom; page 8, right; page 10, left; page 12, top; page 13, top; page 16; page 18; page 22; page 23.

Chris Honeywell (photos of original artwork by Korky Paul): back cover; page 14, bottom right; page 15; page 17, top left; page 23, bottom middle and bottom right.

All other photos, Rupert Horrox.

Thanks to Sue Matthew and the children of St Ebbe's CE Aided First School, Oxford; John Armstrong and the children of Bridgewater School, Berkhamsted; Alan Morgan and the children of Radcliffe-on-Trent Junior School, Nottingham, for their help with all the questions in this book.

Thanks to Korky Paul, Susan Moxley, Zoë Paul and Oska Paul for their patience and co-operation during the making of this book.

Illustrations
Zoë Paul, page 18, bottom.
Oska Paul, page 19, top left.
All other illustrations, Korky Paul.

Illustrations from the following titles are made by permission of Oxford University Press: *Winnie the Witch*, back cover; page 4, page 23. *The Fish Who Could Wish*, page 4. *Dragon Poems*, page 4. *Dinosaur Poems*, page 15. *Sanji and the Baker*, page 14. *Professor Puffendorf's Secret Potions*, page 14. *Captain Teachum's Buried Treasure*, page 14 and page 15. *Magic Poems*, page 23.

Illustration from *The Crocodile and the Dumper Truck,* page 12 and 23, by permission of Sadie Fields Productions Ltd. Illustration from *Say It In English,* page 11, by permission of Efstathiadis Group S.A. Advertisement for Homes Trust Life, page 11.

Heinemann Educational Publishers
Halley Court, Jordan Hill, Oxford OX2 8EJ
a division of Reed Educational & Professional Publishing Ltd

OXFORD FLORENCE PRAGUE MADRID ATHENS MELBOURNE
AUCKLAND KUALA LUMPUR SINGAPORE TOKYO IBADAN
NAIROBI KAMPALA JOHANNESBURG GABORONE PORTSMOUTH
NH (USA) CHICAGO MEXICO CITY SAO PAULO

© Reed Educational & Professional Publishing Ltd 1997

First published 1997

02 01 00 99 98 97

10 9 8 7 6 5 4 3 2 1

British Library Cataloguing in Publication Data
A catalogue record for this book is available from the British Library.

ISBN 0 435 09564 1   *Korky Paul: Biography of an Illustrator:*
                     individual copy pack: 6 copies of 1 title

ISBN 0 435 09415 7   Stage E pack: 1 each of 7 titles

Colour reproduction by Reacta Graphics.

Printed and bound in Great Britain by Scotprint.

Contents

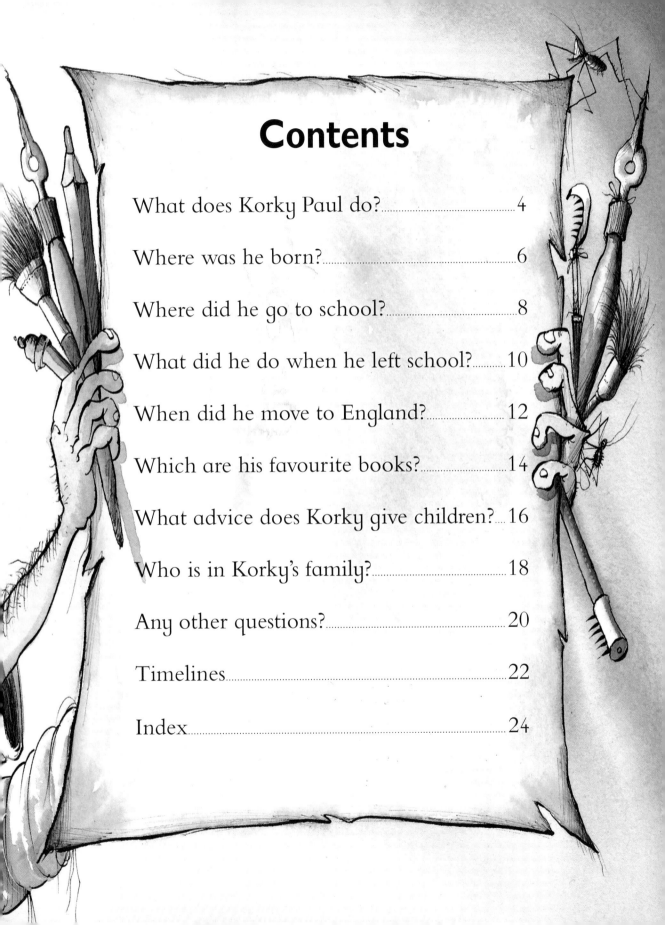

What does Korky Paul do?

Korky Paul in his studio ▲

Korky Paul is an illustrator. He draws pictures of monsters, pirates, professors and witches. He draws pictures for books. Some of the books are famous. Some of the books have won prizes.

Some of Korky's books ▶

Korky's real name is Hamish Vigne Christie Paul.
When he was a child, his nickname was Koektjie
(pronounced 'Cookie'). Korky could not say this
name properly. He put an 'r' in the middle. He has
been called Korky ever since.

Where was he born?

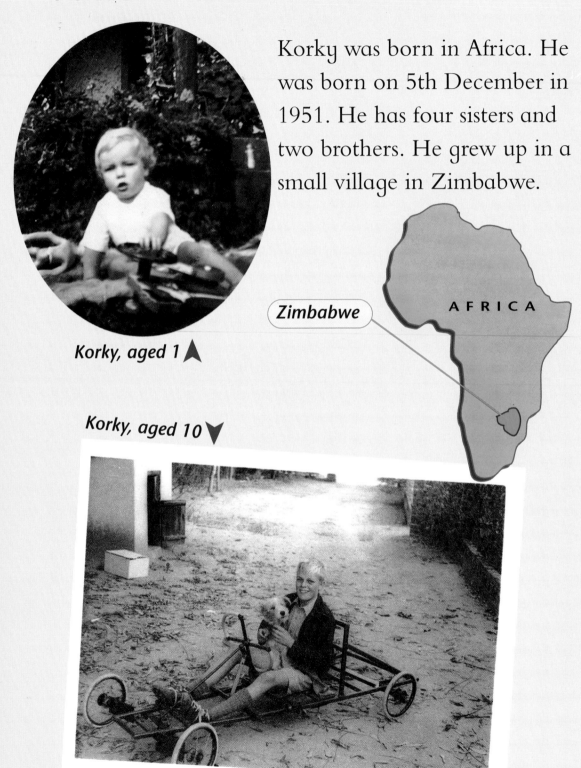

Korky was born in Africa. He was born on 5th December in 1951. He has four sisters and two brothers. He grew up in a small village in Zimbabwe.

Korky, aged 1 ▲

Zimbabwe

AFRICA

Korky, aged 10 ▼

Korky's parents are called Barbara and Denzil. His mum was a nurse. His dad did lots of different jobs. His favourite job was drilling for water.

Family tree ▼

Mum

Dad

William   Brenda   Tessa   Valerie

Korky   Donald   Gale

Korky's mum and dad ◄

Where did he go to school?

SCHOOL *Godfrey Huggins*

TERMINAL REPORT

On *Hamish Paul* for *Third* term, 1959.

Standard I Class No. in Class ... 29

Pupil's Age *8 yrs.* Absent ... 3 ... days

Average Age of Class *8 yrs. 8 mths.* Next Term commences *21st January, 1960.*

ENGLISH *Language and vocabulary :- Very good progress.*
Spelling :- Has greatly improved.
Composition :- Good ideas but more care required in writing.

ARITHMETIC *Tables and Mental Arithmetic :- Good. He has*
improved considerably this term. Mechanical work :- Works
steadily with good results. Problems :- Fair. More effort required.

HISTORY *Good progress.*

GEOGRAPHY *Good progress.* *He has a sound background*
knowledge and shows much

NATURE STUDY *Very good progress.* *interest in these lessons.*

CRAFTWORK *Very good progress. He is clever with his*
hands and shows promise.

SEWING *Writing :- Requires more care and effort.*

ART *Very good. His paintings are original and*
show character.

PHYSICAL TRAINING *Good.*

OTHER SUBJECTS (e.g. Music) *Reading :- Good progress. Composition*
is good but expression could be better.

GENERAL ACTIVITIES *Hamish takes an enthusiastic part in*
school activities. He is learning to swim, and enjoys games.

CLASS TEACHER'S REMARKS *Hamish has been more conscientious this*
term. His English and Arithmetic have improved
considerably. In class he is a pleasant well-liked pupil.

Satisfactory progress.

School report on Korky, aged 8 ▲

Korky, aged 17 ▲

ART ....*Very good .... His paintings are original and*
show character.

Korky went to Godfrey Huggins Junior School in
Zimbabwe. He then went to Estcourt High
School in South Africa. His favourite subjects
were History and Art. He started to draw when
he was five years old.

Korky spent a lot of time drawing. He drew on his pencil boxes and all over his exercise books. When he was a teenager, he drew posters for school dances.

Sketch by Korky, aged 15

What did he do when he left school?

Korky went to Durban Art School in South Africa. He went to the California Institute of Arts in America. He travelled round Europe in a van.

Sketch by Korky, aged 22 ➤

Korky, aged 24 ▲

In 1976, Korky went to Greece. He got a job in an advertising firm. He met an editor called James Watt. James asked him to draw the pictures for a book. The book was called *Say it in English*.

One of Korky's advertisements ▲

Mrs Callas   Athena   Mr Callas

Mrs Stratis   Nikos   Mr Stratis

Korky's first book, published in 1976 ▲

When did he move to England?

Korky and Susan Moxley ▲
in 1980. They were
married in 1983.

Korky moved to England in 1980. He met a man called Ray Marshall. Korky and Ray decided to draw and write a pop-up book for children. The book was called *The Crocodile and the Dumper Truck*.

It was very hot.
Crocodile longed for a swim.
"We'll cool off in the Trafalgar Square fountains,"
said the the Dumper Truck.
"Coo-er! Whatever next?" grumbled a pigeon.

The Crocodile and the Dumper Truck
was published in 1981   ▲

Korky and Ron Heapy, his current editor. They are holding a prize for Winnie the Witch

Now, Korky has drawn the pictures for 45 children's books. He has stopped working in advertising. He works on about three books per year. Each book takes about three months. He draws for eight hours a day. He has won prizes for some of his books.

Korky working on a new book

Which are his favourite books?

My favourite books are *Sanji and the Baker* and *Professor Puffendorf's Secret Potions*. I also enjoyed doing the drawings for *Captain Teachum's Buried Treasure*. I really liked the stories and the characters in these books.

▲ *Korky has drawn himself in this picture*

Korky sometimes puts drawings of his friends into his books. He also puts in characters from other books. There are lots of things to look at in Korky's drawings.

What advice does Korky give children?

If you want to draw pictures for books, you must draw draw draw! You should draw every day. Ask your teacher if you can draw the posters for a school play or concert.

Black and white sketch ▼

Colour artwork ▼

Captain Teachum's
BURIED TREASURE
Korky Paul & Peter Carter.

Finished book!
►

Captain Teachum's
BURIED TREASURE
Korky Paul and Peter Carter

You can look at the
pictures in different books. You can
work hard at your art lessons. You
will develop your own style!

Who is in Korky's family?

Korky and his family ▲

Korky and Susan have two children. They have a daughter called Zoë who is ten years old and a son called Oska who is five years old. They all live together in Oxford.

▲

Picture of her cat, Killer Nutmeg, by Zoë

Korky is 1 metre 83cm tall. He weighs 75 kilos.
He is 45 years old. He has blond hair and
blue eyes.

**Portrait of Korky
by Oska**

Any other questions?

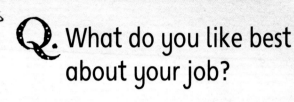

Q. What do you like best about your job?

A. Being the Boss!

Q. What have been the best moments in your life?

A. When our children were born.

Q. Do you like climbing trees?

A. Of course.

Q. Do you wear glasses?

A. Yes for driving or watching movies and T.V.

Q. Do you enjoy your job?

A. I love it.

Q. How many times a week do you take a shower?

A. Ten times.

◄ *Korky with his favourite things*

21

Timelines

Korky's life

Aged 24

Aged 17

Aged 1

1952   **1968**   **1975**

Korky's pictures

Korky has grown up. He now has a family. He has drawn the pictures for lots of books. Do you think his drawing style has changed?

Sketch, aged 15   Sketch, aged 22

1966   **1973**

Aged 29

Aged 44

Aged 45

1980   *1995*   *1997*

The Crocodile and the
Dumper Truck, **aged 30**

Winnie the Witch,
aged 36

Magic Poems,
aged 45

1981   *1987*   *1997*

What do you think Korky will do next?

Index

a
b
c
d
e
f
g
h
i
j
k
l
m
n
o
p
q
r
s
t
u
v
w
x
y
z